LeapFrog SchoolHouse™

TURBO TWIST®
Spelling
Teacher's Manual

Table of Contents

Y0-DDP-492

TURBO TWIST® SPELLING SCOPE AND SEQUENCE: CARTRIDGE MAP

TURBO TWIST Spelling from LeapFrog SchoolHouse provides comprehensive practice of spelling skills for grades 1 through 6. The educator-approved curriculum on TURBO TWIST Spelling can be accessed either by inserting one of the supplemental learning cartridges or by exploring the 33 levels that come pre-built into the device itself. The following scope and sequence charts show a level-by-level breakdown of spelling skills and sample words included on the TURBO TWIST Spelling cartridges. For a descriptive breakdown of what's on the device itself, see page 34.

Grade 1 (on grade 1/grade 2 cartridge)

Skill Level	Key Spelling Skills	Sample Words
1	Words with Short a	hat
2	Words with Short e	met
3	Words with Short i	fin
4	Words with Short o and Short i	jog
5	Words with Short o	mop
6	Words with Short u	hug
7	Consonant Blends with s	slim
8	Consonant Blends with l	plan
9	Consonant Blends with l and r	crop
10	Consonant Blends with r and Words with Long a	fade
11	Words with Long a	plane
12	Words with Long e	feed
13	Words with Long e and Words with Long i	dine
14	Words with Long i	pride
15	Words with Long o	joke
16	Words with Long u	prune
17	Words with Long u and Words That End in ck	kick
18	Words That End in ck	tack
19	Words That Are Not Spelled the Way They Sound	of
20	Consonant Combination sh and Words That Are Not Spelled the Way They Sound	hush
21	Consonant Combination th	than
22	Consonant Combinations ch, tch	ditch
23	Words That End with st or nd	rust
24	More Words That Are Not Spelled the Way They Sound	been
25	Adding ed or ing to Words	going
26	Adding ed or ing to Words	wished
27	Adding s or es to Words	dogs
28	Adding s or es to Words and More Words with Long a	clay
29	More Words with Long a and Long i	fry
30	More Words That Are Not Spelled the Way They Sound	sure
31	More Words with Long o	owe
32	Words with the ow Sound	cow
33	Words for Color and Size	green
34	Words for Family and Friends	father
35	Words with Short a, e and i	tap
36	Words with Short o or Short u	gum

Grade 2 (on grade 1/grade 2 cartridge)

Skill Level	Key Spelling Skills	Sample Words
37	Consonant Blends with r or l	milk
38	Consonant Combinations sh, th, ch, and tch	cloth
39	Consonant Blends ng and nk	sink
40	Words with a Double Consonant at the End	boss
41	Words for Numbers	nine
42	Words That Are Not Spelled the Way They Sound	key
43	Words with the k Sound and Words That Are Not Spelled the Way They Sound	kiss
44	Words with Long a and Words That Are Not Spelled the Way They Sound	made
45	Words with Long e	eat
46	Words with Long i and Long o	try
47	Words with Long o	show
48	Words That Begin with qu or squ and Words with the oo sound in toot	quest
49	Compound Words	airplane
50	Adding ed or ing to Words	liked
51	Adding s, es or -ing to Words	flashes
52	More Words That Are Not Spelled the Way They Sound	minute
53	Consonant Combination wh	whisker
54	Words with the ar Sound	smart
55	Words with the or Sound	sport
56	More Words with a Double Consonant at the End	shell
57	Homophones (Words That Sound the Same)	fare/fair
58	Two-Syllable Words with Short Vowels	insect
59	More Compound Words	popcorn
60	Consonant Combinations mp, ck, nd	damp
61	Words with the ow Sound	proud
62	Words with the oy Sound	choice
63	Words with the oy Sound	joyful
64	Words with the oy Sound and Words for Parts of the Body	ankle
65	Words with Short u	study
66	More Compound Words	moonlight
67	More Compound Words and Consonant Combinations sh, th, ch, and tch	depth

Scope and Sequence, *continued*

Grade 3 (on grade 3/grade 4 cartridge)

Skill Level	Key Spelling Skills	Sample Words
1	Three-Letter Consonant Blends	march
2	Three-Letter Consonant Blends	strum
3	Words with Long a	chase
4	Words with Long e	speech
5	Words with Long i	scribe
6	Words with Long o and Long i	elbow
7	Words with the Vowel Sound in book, hoop, or huge and Words with Long o	brook
8	Words That End with the j or s Sound	fudge
9	Words That End with the j or s Sound	slice
10	Words with the er and aw Sound	splinter
11	Words with the aw Sound	drawer
12	Compound Words	butterfly
13	Words That Are Not Spelled the Way They Sound	every
14	Words with the ar Sound and Words Not Spelled the Way They Sound	guard
15	Words with the ar Sound	heart
16	Words with the or Sound	explore
17	Words with the ur Sound	curve
18	Words for Communities and Community Workers	firefighter
19	More Words for Communities and Community Workers	nurse
20	More Consonant Blends and Combinations	grumpy
21	Words with Silent k or Silent w	knock
22	Words with the ow or oy Sound	loyalty
23	Words with a Double Consonant in the Middle	million
24	Words with a Double Consonant in the Middle	carrot
25	Words with a Double Consonant Followed by y	hobby
26	Words with a Double Consonant Followed by y and Adding er or est to Adjectives	bravest
27	Adding ed, ing, or est to Words	funniest
28	Adding ed, ing, or est to Words and Unusual Plurals	chimneys
29	Unusual Plurals	patches
30	More Consonant Blends and Combinations	shrimp
31	Adding er or est to Adjectives	lazier
32	Words with the prefix re-, Consonant Blends and Combinations	rewrite

Grade 4 (on grade 3/grade 4 cartridge)

Skill Level	Key Spelling Skills	Sample Words
33	Words with Long i	frighten
34	Words with Long o and Long i	decode
35	Words with the Vowel Sound in book, hoop, or huge	mushroom
36	Adding ed or ing to Words	married
37	Adding er or est to Words	happiest
38	Words with the oi or ow Sound, Adding est to Words	safest
39	Homophones (Words That Sound the Same)	heal/heel
40	Adding s or es to Words	coaches
41	Unusual Plurals	geese
42	Words with the ar or air Sound, Unusual Plurals	dairy
43	Words with the or and air Sound	forecast
44	Words with the ur Sound	earth
45	Words with the eer and ur Sound	fears
46	Words with the j and eer Sound	gymnastic
47	Words with the Unstressed uh Sound	conduct
48	Words for Holidays and Celebrations and Unstressed uh Sound	celebration
49	Compound Words and Words for Holidays and Celebrations	bluebird
50	Compound Words	teaspoon
51	Words with the Unstressed uh Sound and l or r	nickel
52	Words with the Unstressed uh Sound and n	chicken
53	Words with the aw and the Unstressed uh Sound	caught
54	Three-Syllable Words	harmony
55	Three-Syllable Words	sensitive
56	Words That Are Not Spelled the Way They Sound	height
57	Words in Which c Makes the s Sound and Homophones	lettuce
58	More Homophones	overdue/overdo
59	Words with the Prefix mis-, dis-, in-, un-, or re-	misplace
60	Words with the Suffix -ful or -less	respectful
61	Names of States	Minnesota
62	Words with the Suffix -ness, -ment, or -ly	development
63	Words with Silent Letters	comb
64	Words with Silent Letters and Words from Geography	delta
65	Words from Geography	peninsula
66	Words with Short Vowels	glint
67	Words with Long a, e, i or o	danger
68	More Words with Long a, e, i or o	hydrogen

Scope and Sequence, *continued*

Grade 5 (on grade 5/grade 6 cartridge)

Skill Level	Key Spelling Skills	Sample Words
1	Words with Long i or Long o	cyclone
2	Words with Long i or Long o and Words with the Vowel Sound in huge	amuse
3	Words with the oo Sound in hoop, or huge	produce
4	Words with the aw, oi, or ow Sound	lawful
5	Words with the air, ar, or or Sound	heirloom
6	Words with the ur or eer Sound	murmur
7	Words with the Unstressed uh Sound	effective
8	Words with the Unstressed uh Sound Followed by l, n, or r	cannon
9	Compound Words	classmate
10	Words with the sh or ch Sound	furniture
11	Words with the k Sound, the s Sound, or the j Sound	chemical
12	Words with the f or j Sound	dolphin
13	Words with the f Sound	paragraph
14	Words for the Universe	comet
15	Homophones (Words That Sound the Same)	groan/grown
16	Words with the Prefix pre-, re-, post-, or co-	precaution
17	Words with the Prefix dis-, in-, im-, non-, or un-	disinfect
18	Words with the Prefix bi-, mid-, semi-, or tri-	midnight
19	Words with ie or ei	receipt
20	Words That Are Not Spelled the Way They Sound	chocolate
21	Adding er, est, ed, or ing to Words	cozier
22	Words with the Suffix -ful, -less, -ment, or -ness	friendliness
23	Words with the Suffix -ion, -tion, -sion, or -ess	decision
24	Words with the Suffix -ion, -tion, or -sion	protection
25	Words with the Suffix -ent, -ant, -able, or -ible	radiant
26	Words from American Government	preamble
27	Three-Syllable and Four-Syllable Words	especially
28	Unusual Plurals	halves
29	Names of Flowers	geranium
30	Words about Creatures and Flowers	omnivore
31	Words with a Greek or Latin Root	centimeter
32	Short Vowels	involve

Grade 6 (on grade 5/grade 6 cartridge)

Skill Level	Key Spelling Skills	Sample Words
33	Short Vowels	enemy
34	Long a and Long e	concrete
35	Long i and Long o	oboe
36	Words with the Vowel Sound in hoop or huge	cocoon
37	Words with the Vowel Sound in hoop or huge	juice
38	Compound Words	headquarters
39	r-Controlled Vowels	gorgeous
40	Words with the Unstressed uh Sound	elevate
41	Words with the Unstressed uh Sound Followed by r	molar
42	Words with the Unstressed uh Sound Followed by n or l	cymbal
43	Homophones	medal/metal
44	Adding -ed and -ing	occurring
45	Plurals	embargoes
46	Consonant Blends and Combinations	government
47	Words with the f Sound, the z Sound, or the zh Sound in fusion	laser
48	Words for the Distant Past	ancient
49	Double Consonants	blizzard
50	Endings ion, tion, sion	commission
51	Suffixes -ent, -ant, -able, -ible, or -ion	diligent
52	Suffixes -ance, -ence, -ate, or able	convenience
53	Words for the Performing Arts	baritone
54	Words for the Performing Arts	musician
55	Spelling the sh Sound	initial
56	Prefixes super-, sub-, inter-, intra-	subterranean
57	Negative Prefixes	discontinue
58	Prefixes per-, pre-, pro-	presume
59	Words for Law and Government	federal
60	More Compound Words	markdown
61	More Compound Words	withhold
62	Words from Greek or Latin	epidermis
63	Words from Other Languages	kayak
64	Words That Are Not Spelled the Way They Sound	technical
65	Words for Commerce	profit
66	More Prefixes	adjust
67	More Prefixes	midterm
68	More Suffixes	fortitude

Introduction to TURBO TWIST® Spelling

WHY USE THIS PRODUCT?

TURBO TWIST Spelling is a versatile learning tool that helps students achieve and master important spelling skills. This educational tool offers motivating, engaging, and interactive practice exercises that include unique graphics and sound effects. TURBO TWIST Spelling is tailored to specific grade and skill levels to provide individualized spelling practice. It assesses and adapts the learning path based on individual needs.

With TURBO TWIST Spelling, your students can practice using short vowel sounds, consonant blends, consonant digraphs, and other important spelling skills. The same sequence of spelling skills learned in the classroom can be reinforced with TURBO TWIST Spelling. It uses core spelling words, enabling your students to develop and apply essential spelling skills at each grade level. Fundamental spelling rules are practiced using TURBO TWIST Spelling to encourage and involve your students. In this way, TURBO TWIST Spelling can be an integral part of every student's learning experience.

Within the first few minutes of use, TURBO TWIST Spelling analyzes your students' spelling abilities. Then, it continually adjusts as your students advance. As a result, your students are able to constantly work at the skill level appropriate to them and progress at their own pace. This pacing creates an engaging learning environment that will prevent your students from becoming frustrated by questions that are too difficult or bored by questions that are too easy. This unique feature will reactivate each time your students use the TURBO TWIST Spelling, unless they manually adjust the level.

BENEFITS

Unlike ordinary skill and drill practice sheets, TURBO TWIST Spelling is an interactive reinforcement tool that engages all learners in beneficial practice activities. Your students can effectively use TURBO TWIST Spelling individually and in small groups to practice spelling without direct support from you. If a student finishes an assignment early, TURBO TWIST Spelling can be used to sustain and strengthen spelling skills, or a small group of students can practice together by using the multiplayer mode.

Individualization. Because your students can choose their own level of play, they are always engaged in meaningful and rewarding practice. The auto-leveling feature can also determine the students' spelling levels and alter content to meet individual ability.

Positive Experience. The continuous positive verbal and pictorial reinforcement on TURBO TWIST Spelling will boost your students' confidence levels, resulting in noticeable improvement.

Feedback. TURBO TWIST Spelling can track your students' progress to help you assess their strengths and weaknesses. When a student turns on TURBO TWIST Spelling and inputs his or her user name, TURBO TWIST Spelling begins tracking that student's assessment information.

Home Connection. In addition to being a helpful classroom tool, TURBO TWIST Spelling can also be utilized at home to continue establishing and expanding important spelling skills. Students can practice the same spelling skills at home that they are learning in the classroom by simply selecting the appropriate level on TURBO TWIST Spelling. TURBO TWIST Spelling offers several study modes, each providing motivating and reinforcing spelling practice. Both at home and in the classroom, students can practice spelling skills with TURBO TWIST spelling.

RATIONALE, GOALS, AND RESEARCH BEHIND TURBO TWIST SPELLING

Skill Level Assimilation.
TURBO TWIST Spelling questions are arranged into skill levels based on an educator-approved curriculum for grades 1 through 6. Educators know that students learn best when instruction matches skill level. TURBO TWIST cartridges have been developed by educational experts and aligned with state standards to help expand students' skills and growing knowledge base with exciting grade-specific content. Students' skill levels are continuously monitored, and the pace of skill introduction is adjusted accordingly.

A Multisensory Approach.
TURBO TWIST Spelling fosters learning success through a hands-on, multisensory approach. When your students use it as a practice tool, they read words spelled on the screen, hear positive feedback and musical sounds, and use their hands to manipulate the Letter Dial and push the Slam Button. This visual, auditory, and kinesthetic approach will grab and hold your students' attention. When your students use TURBO TWIST Spelling, they will be engaged in the activity, and the device features will help them stay on task. And TURBO TWIST Spelling provides students with a great deal of control. Your students will feel in charge of their own learning, which is intrinsically motivating.

Encouragement for Students.
TURBO TWIST Spelling offers immediate feedback after each spelling question, facilitating the learning process while enhancing self-confidence. Rather than telling students that they are wrong, TURBO TWIST Spelling delivers positive prompts encouraging them to try again. Students are then shown how to spell the word correctly.

Variety in Learning.
Your students can use TURBO TWIST Spelling to review and practice vowel sounds, consonant combinations, homophones, words with silent letters, prefixes, and suffixes. The multimodal quality of TURBO TWIST Spelling is compelling for students of all ages. The five study modes are presented in both visual and auditory form. **Learn It!** teaches your students how to spell in a style similar to flash cards. **Missing Letter** encourages your students to fill in the missing letters of words in order to score points. **Spell It!** prompts students to fill in all the letters of a word and score big points. **Secret Word** asks your students to guess the correct letters to spell the secret word. **MultiPlayer** allows two to four players to take turns spelling entire words.

Continued Practice.
You and your students will find TURBO TWIST Spelling very user-friendly. This product provides an extremely well-sequenced spelling curriculum balanced among the core spelling skills. Your students receive constant guidance, as well as feedback on their responses. Numerous case studies from educators have shown that time on task, high expectations, and multiple methods for question solving done through a multisensory approach are highly effective teaching strategies. More about these studies can be found at our LeapFrog SchoolHouse Web site (**www.leapfrogschoolhouse.com**). TURBO TWIST Spelling is a uniquely efficient instructional tool that invites you and your students to put these time-proven practices into effect.

Introduction to TURBO TWIST® Spelling, *continued*

AUDIO ASSISTANCE

TURBO TWIST® Spelling includes a headphone jack so your students can use headphones. This way they won't disturb classmates working on assignments, projects, or other TURBO TWIST Spelling practice modes. Using headphones will greatly decrease noise level within your classroom, providing a positive learning environment for everyone. In addition, TURBO TWIST Spelling volume control buttons raise and lower the volume. This, too, can help your students practice quietly.

The Repeat Button may be used if your students need directions or questions repeated. This feature is especially beneficial for ELL students and students with special learning needs who may need directions and questions repeated several times in order to answer successfully.

TURBO TWIST Spelling clearly reads all prompts, such as directions, questions, and answers, for your students to follow. This allows students with limited reading skills to work through exercises with little difficulty, as fun and inviting voices lead them through all activities. Auditory praise boosts students' confidence levels and motivates them to continue using TURBO TWIST Spelling.

If students are unable to answer a question correctly when practicing, the correct answer is given to them, preventing students from practicing errors. The audio assistance features makes TURBO TWIST Spelling a useful tool for all kinds of learners.

SPECIAL EDUCATION/ENGLISH LANGUAGE LEARNERS

TURBO TWIST Spelling can be an asset to any teacher or parent working with students with special learning needs, including English language learners. Just as TURBO TWIST Spelling allows all students to individualize their practice and work at their own pace, it provides students with special needs unique tools for improving their spelling skills.

Through its combined visual/auditory/ tactile support system, TURBO TWIST Spelling helps to meet the learning needs of students who respond best to different teaching approaches. Since TURBO TWIST Spelling's screen displays fun graphics, game modes, learning levels, and spelling words, visual learners will find the device accessible and easy-to-use. Auditory learners will benefit from the vocalized instructions for using the device, oral praise for correct answers, read-aloud letters and spelling words, and meaningful sound effects. And for those students who learn best through hands-on activities, TURBO TWIST Spelling's tactile requirements—spinning the Letter Dial to choose letters, "slamming" the Slam Button to input choices, and maneuvering through the activities with the Directional Arrows Button—will hold interest. In all cases, TURBO TWIST Spelling lessens student intimidation by providing a welcoming, user-friendly interface.

Since TURBO TWIST Spelling supports the special needs of various types of learners, most students will be able to use it for spelling practice even without teacher assistance. In addition to incorporating different learning styles, TURBO TWIST Spelling works for students with very different spelling abilities. The target spelling words cover a wide range of difficulty levels, from simple consonant-vowel-consonant words (*cat*) to complex irregular spellings of much harder words (*circuitry*). TURBO TWIST Spelling both tracks student performance and gives students the option of setting their own learning levels; as a result, students with very diverse spelling skills can use the device successfully.

One of the more common types of students with special learning needs, English language learners can use TURBO TWIST Spelling to reinforce their English-language development through the practice of spelling skills. Since TURBO TWIST Spelling reads aloud the text displayed on the screen, students both hear and read correctly spelled English words. This has three effects: it enables English language learners to understand the TURBO TWIST Spelling directions, helps students associate spoken English with written text, and teaches students how to spell and read English words correctly. Also, you can pair ELL students with English-speaking students to help bridge the gap between the two.

For all these reasons, TURBO TWIST Spelling is a great tool for helping students with special learning needs thrive in a classroom setting. Its multisensory approach and multiple-level offering can help all your students—regardless of learning style, skill level, or previous experience with spelling in English—succeed in mastering spelling skills.

GETTING STARTED WITH TURBO TWIST® SPELLING

Built-in Features

On/Off Button Students turn on TURBO TWIST Spelling by pushing the blue On/Off Button. They are immediately greeted by a friendly voice welcoming them to TURBO TWIST Spelling. Turbo introduces himself as the host. (If the device is left untouched for one minute, it will shut off automatically to conserve battery power.)

Volume Adjust Buttons Students press the blue, triangle-shaped buttons to control volume. The plus button (+) increases volume, and the minus button (–) lowers volume.

Games Button Students can press the Games Button to choose different study modes. Each time they hit this button, a new mode title will be announced and displayed. See "Study Modes" for a description of each mode.

Repeat Button Students press the Repeat Button to repeat the last question or answer.

Directional Arrows Button Students use the Directional Arrows Button to make selections. For example, when Turbo is asking students to choose a mode, he instructs them to use the right arrow, and each time this arrow is pressed, a new mode is listed on the display and announced. Pressing the other arrows will help students move back and forth between mode choices.

Letter Dial The Letter Dial contains all 26 letters of the alphabet. Students turn the Letter Dial to select letters when spelling words.

Slam Button Students press the large Slam Button on the end to enter answers, confirm commands, or jump to the next question.

Headphone Jack At the back of TURBO TWIST Spelling, there is a headphone jack for quiet play. It accepts 1/8″ plugs, but other sizes can be used along with an adapter.

Cartridge Slot At the side of this handheld, there is a sliding door covering a cartridge slot. Slide the door open to insert a TURBO TWIST Spelling cartridge, which can be used to add spelling words.

Battery Compartment A screwdriver is needed to replace batteries. Loosen the screw on the battery compartment panel. Remove the panel and insert four AA batteries. Replace the panel and tighten the screw.

Study Modes

TURBO TWIST Spelling motivates students and holds their attention with animation, music, and sound effects. Whichever learning mode students choose—Learn It!, Missing Letter, Spell It!, Secret Word, or MultiPlayer—TURBO TWIST Spelling offers an engaging and rewarding educational experience.

Learn It! TURBO TWIST Spelling allows students to see and hear how a new word is spelled. First, TURBO TWIST Spelling asks how to spell a certain word. One blank underline is shown for each letter in that word. Students hit the Slam Button to see and hear how that word is spelled.

Missing Letter TURBO TWIST Spelling spells out a word, but omits some letters. It's the student's job to fill in those missing letters by turning the Letter Dial and then hitting the Slam Button. This mode playfully offers hints when a player is having trouble. TURBO TWIST Spelling also presents sample sentences for many of the spelling words in this mode.

Spell It! TURBO TWIST Spelling challenges students to spell an entire word. In this mode, TURBO TWIST Spelling will announce a new word and show students how many letters are in that word. Students then fill in blank underlines by turning the Letter Dial and hitting the Slam Button. This mode offers hints if a player is having trouble.

Secret Word TURBO TWIST® Spelling challenges students to guess the correct letters to spell a secret word. At first, this mode shows only blank underlines for each of the letters in the secret word so students can see the number of letters they are trying to find. Students begin turning the Letter Dial and hitting the Slam Button to guess a letter. If students are successful in finding a missing letter, that letter is inserted into one of the blank underlines on the screen. Students proceed until they find all the letters.

MultiPlayer This mode is for groups of two, three, or four students. Students take turns filling in all the letters to spell entire words. Students play a total of six rounds and compete for "brain cells." The student with the most brain cells at the end of the sixth round wins.

Selecting a User Name

When students first turn on TURBO TWIST Spelling, they will select user names. This user name helps TURBO TWIST Spelling track a student's progress and assign him or her the appropriate level to play.

TURBO TWIST Spelling adjusts the level to the ideal level of challenge based on the individual student's previous correct or incorrect answers. Students can also adjust the level manually at the start of a game by using the up and down Directional Arrows.

Now that you know the basics, you and your students are on your way to an engaging and exciting learning experience.

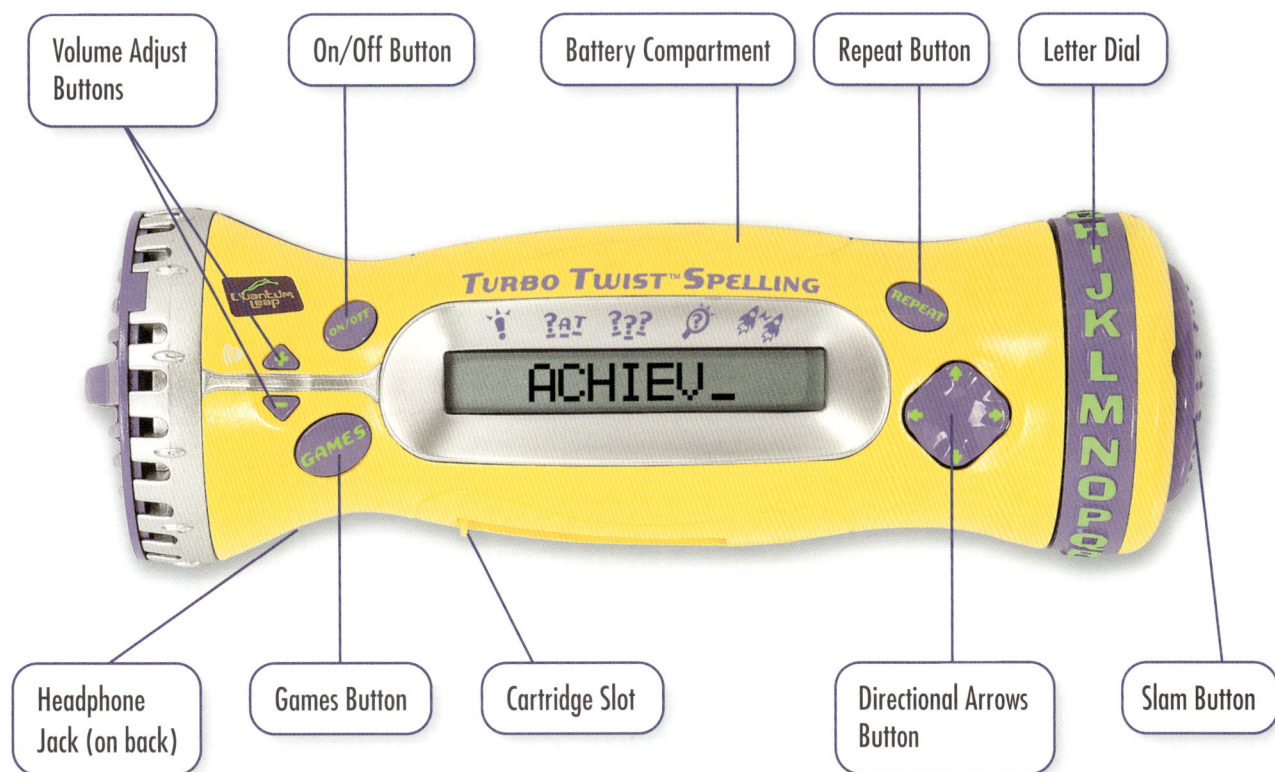

Volume Adjust Buttons

On/Off Button

Battery Compartment

Repeat Button

Letter Dial

Headphone Jack (on back)

Games Button

Cartridge Slot

Directional Arrows Button

Slam Button

TURBO TWIST™ SPELLING

ACHIEV_

Introduction to TURBO TWIST® Spelling, *continued*

HOW TO PLAY

TURBO TWIST® Spelling offers various games that will keep your students interested. Students can learn from five different study modes.

Learn It! TURBO TWIST Spelling allows students to hear and see how a new word is spelled.

1. Students press the right arrow on the Directional Arrows Button when prompted or the Games Button to display mode choices. When "Learn It!" appears, they press the Slam Button to start learning.

2. TURBO TWIST Spelling selects a word from the student's skill level. The number of letters in that word is displayed with blank underlines. Students then hit the Slam Button to see and hear how that word is spelled.

3. After the word is spelled completely, students are prompted to press the Slam Button to move on to another word. Remember, students can press the Repeat Button if they'd like to hear a question again.

4. If students want to change the difficulty level of the words, they can press the up arrow and then use the up and down arrows to adjust the level. The Slam Button is then pressed to confirm the new skill level.

Missing Letter Students fill in missing letters to spell level-appropriate words.

1. Students press the Games Button or the right arrow on the Directional Arrows Button to display study mode choices. When "Missing Letter" appears, pressing the Slam Button starts this mode.

2. TURBO TWIST Spelling selects a word from the student's skill level. A word with letters missing is shown.

3. Students turn the Letter Dial to find a missing letter in the word on the screen and then hit the Slam Button to enter their choice. If the student is correct, TURBO TWIST Spelling moves on to the next missing letter. If the student selects the wrong letter, TURBO TWIST Spelling offers a hint.

4. When a word is spelled correctly, students know immediately from the triumphant sound of the music. To move to the next word, students press the Slam Button.

Spell It! Students are challenged to spell whole words.

1. Students press the Games Button or the right arrow on the Directional Arrows Button to display mode choices. Pressing the Slam Button when "Spell It!" appears starts this mode.

2. TURBO TWIST Spelling presents a level-appropriate word, and the display shows the number of letters in that word. Students turn the Letter Dial to select the first letter, then press the Slam Button. They are then encouraged to select the next letters until the whole word is complete.

3. After each word is spelled, students hit the Slam Button to move on to the next word.

Secret Word Students are challenged to guess the correct letters to spell a secret word.

1. The student presses the Games Button or the right arrow on the Directional Arrows Button to display game choices. When "Secret Word" appears, the student hits the Slam Button to select the mode.

2. At first, the display shows only blank underlines for each of the letters in the secret word. Students must guess a letter in the secret word by turning the Letter Dial and then pressing the Slam Button.

3. If the selected letter is part of the secret word, it will appear in the correct spot in the word.

4. After students have successfully discovered all the letters of the secret word, the student hits the Slam Button to move on to the next word.

MultiPlayer This lively game is designed for groups of two, three, or four students who are looking for a good challenge. Students spell words to compete for "brain cells."

1. Students press the Games Button or the right arrow on the Directional Arrows Button to display mode choices. To activate, students press the Slam Button when "MultiPlayer" appears.

2. Students select the number of players by pressing the up arrow to choose two, three, or four players. Students press the Slam Button to enter their choice.

3. Students choose the desired level of play by pressing the up and down arrows and then hitting the Slam Button.

4. The first player gets a word to spell. That student turns the Letter Dial to choose a letter. Then, he or she hits the Slam Button to enter the chosen letter. The student continues to find and select each letter in the word until the whole word is spelled out.

5. "Brain cells" are accumulated by students when they spell words correctly. If a student spells a word incorrectly during a round of play, TURBO TWIST® Spelling will show the student how to spell the word.

6. Once the first student has spelled out his or her word, TURBO TWIST Spelling instructs the student to pass it to the next student. Then, the second student is asked to spell a word.

7. At the midpoint in the game, TURBO TWIST Spelling gives students the current score.

8. After six rounds of play, the student with the most "brain cells" wins the gold medal.

Super Sentences

LEARNING OBJECTIVES

- to write and practice spelling
- to use words in context

SKILLS PRACTICED

- spelling
- word comprehension
- sentence writing

MATERIALS NEEDED

- TURBO TWIST® Spelling
- several sheets of writing paper
- pencils
- timer

PREPARATION

Students should have writing paper, pencils, and TURBO TWIST Spelling.

PREP TIME

5 minutes

DURATION OF ACTIVITY

5–25 minutes

SKILL LEVEL

Beginner

PLAYERS

1–4

DIRECTIONS

1. Have students choose the Learn It! mode on TURBO TWIST Spelling.

2. Students then can select an appropriate skill level on TURBO TWIST Spelling.

3. Have students write on a sheet of paper the first five words that TURBO TWIST Spelling gives them.

4. After students have written down five words, check their spellings. If they are correct, set the timer for students to start writing Super Sentences. Select the amount of time depending on your students' ability levels. Five to seven minutes is a good place to start. You can adjust the timer in subsequent games as needed.

5. When the timer starts, have students write five sentences, each containing one of the TURBO TWIST Spelling words that they wrote down. Help students check their sentences to make sure they are complete, begin with a capital letter, and have correct punctuation. Encourage students to double-check the spelling of the words in their sentences against their original spellings.

6. Invite students to share their sentences with each other.

VARIATIONS

- Expand the activity so that students spell more than five words and write more than five sentences.

- Have students work with partners to write their sentences.

- Eliminate the time restriction and have students use between five and ten words from TURBO TWIST Spelling in a long paragraph.

- Challenge students to choose a higher skill level when they retrieve words from Learn It!

Tell Me a Story

LEARNING OBJECTIVE

- to use spelling words correctly when writing

SKILLS PRACTICED

- basic spelling skills
- word comprehension
- sentence writing
- story writing

MATERIALS NEEDED

- TURBO TWIST® Spelling
- several sheets of writing paper
- pencils

PREPARATION

Make sure all students have writing paper, pencils, and TURBO TWIST Spelling.

PREP TIME

5 minutes

DURATION OF ACTIVITY

30 minutes

SKILL LEVEL

All levels

PLAYERS

2–4

DIRECTIONS

1. Have students select the Spell It! mode on TURBO TWIST Spelling.

2. Help students select an appropriate skill level.

3. Then, have each student use TURBO TWIST Spelling to spell between five and ten words and write them correctly on a sheet of paper.

4. When all students have finished, ask a volunteer to write a sentence using one word from his or her list on a clean sheet of paper. Explain that this sentence will begin an add-on story.

5. The volunteer should then pass this sheet of paper to the next student, who will add a sentence to the story, using a word from his or her list.

6. Have students take turns until all students have used all their spelling words.

7. Encourage the group to create a reasonable story—but point out that as they run out of spelling words, it might become harder to come up with sentences that fit the story! Mention that they will have to get creative to finish their story in a way that makes sense.

VARIATIONS

- Provide a theme for the add-on story. Encourage students to be creative in how they fit their words into the theme of the story.

- Before playing, have each group come up with a theme for its story.

- Add a time limit so that students are challenged to think on their feet to add their sentences quickly.

Lesson Plan
Spell It! Mode

Leaping Lily Pads

LEARNING OBJECTIVE
- to spell words

SKILL PRACTICED
- core spelling skills

MATERIALS NEEDED
- TURBO TWIST® Spelling
- several sheets of writing paper
- pencils
- a copy of the Leaping Lily Pads Game Board (page 26) for each pair of students
- one game piece per student

PREPARATION
Make a copy of the Leaping Lily Pads Game Board on page 26 for each pair of students. You might choose to laminate the boards and keep them for extended use. Help students find a game piece to use. Also provide students with scratch paper, pencils, and TURBO TWIST Spelling.

PREP TIME
5–10 minutes

DURATION OF ACTIVITY
25–35 minutes

SKILL LEVEL
Beginner/Intermediate

PLAYERS
2

DIRECTIONS

1. Have students choose the Spell It! mode and an appropriate skill level on TURBO TWIST Spelling.

2. Have Player 1 begin to spell using the Spell It! mode, while Player 2 makes a tally mark on a sheet of paper for each word Player 1 spells correctly on the first try.

3. When Player 1 misses a word, his or her spelling turn is over. Invite Player 1 to finish the turn by moving his or her game piece on the Leaping Lily Pads Game Board, one space for each tally mark earned. Point out to players that they have to follow the directions written on the lily pad that their marker lands on.

4. After Player 1's turn is over, Player 2 takes a turn. The game continues with the players taking turns until one of them reaches Bubba's Buggy Diner at the end of the path on the Leaping Lily Pads Game Board.

VARIATION

- Have two students form a team to challenge another two-student team.

Build a Robot

LEARNING OBJECTIVES

- to spell words correctly
- to use core spelling skills and rules

SKILL PRACTICED

- basic spelling concepts

MATERIALS NEEDED

- TURBO TWIST® Spelling
- a copy of the Build a Robot sheet (page 27) for each student
- pencils

PREPARATION

Make a copy of the Build a Robot sheet on page 27 for each student.

PREP TIME

5 minutes

DURATION OF ACTIVITY

10–20 minutes

SKILL LEVEL

Beginner/Intermediate

PLAYERS

2–4

DIRECTIONS

1. Have students choose the Missing Letter mode on TURBO TWIST Spelling.

2. Help students select an appropriate skill level.

3. Ask all students to begin playing Missing Letter at the same time. Remind them that for each new word, TURBO TWIST Spelling allows only three chances to fill in the missing letter(s). Tell students that any letters selected incorrectly need to be listed at the bottom of the Build a Robot sheet.

4. For each incorrect letter a student chooses, he or she should add one body part to the robot on the Build a Robot sheet.

5. Each student's game ends when he or she has made eight incorrect choices and has built an entire robot. The winner is the student who does not finish his or her robot.

VARIATION

- Have students play several games independently, challenging themselves to increase the number of words they spell correctly before building the robot.

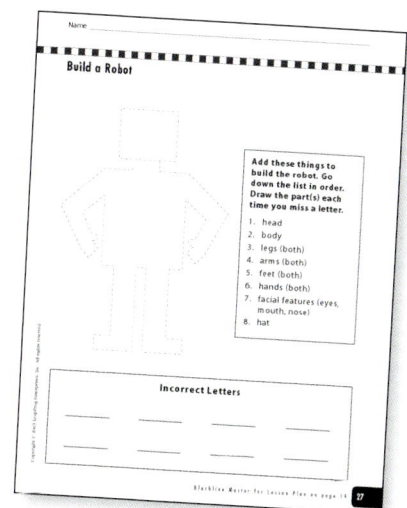

Lesson Plan
Missing Letter Mode

Cut and Choose

LEARNING OBJECTIVES

- to practice spelling words
- to spell words using a limited number of letters

SKILLS PRACTICED

- spelling basic words
- letter identification

MATERIALS NEEDED

- TURBO TWIST® Spelling
- a copy of the Cut and Choose sheet (page 28) for each student
- scissors

PREPARATION

Make a copy of the Cut and Choose sheet on page 28 for each student.

PREP TIME

5 minutes

DURATION OF ACTIVITY

10–25 minutes

SKILL LEVEL

Beginner

PLAYERS

2

DIRECTIONS

1. Have students cut apart the letters on the Cut and Choose page. Instruct students to place all their letters face up.

2. Tell students to choose the Missing Letter mode on TURBO TWIST Spelling. Then help them select an appropriate level.

3. When TURBO TWIST Spelling gives the first Missing Letter word, have Player 1 choose the missing letter(s) from the Cut and Choose letters. Then, invite him or her to key in the missing letter(s) on TURBO TWIST Spelling. If the letters are correct, have Player 1 keep those letters. Any chosen letters that are not part of the Missing Letter word get returned to the student's set of face-up letters.

4. Instruct students to switch players after spelling a word, correctly or incorrectly.

5. Have students play until each student has collected ten letters. Then, challenge students to create a new word with their ten letters. Encourage students to use as many letters as possible.

6. Have students use their new words to challenge each other. Tell students to line up the Cut and Choose cutouts of their new words with a few letters turned face down. Ask students to guess each other's new words.

VARIATION

- Have students write the missing letter(s) on the chalkboard, chart paper, or dry-erase board. Then, have them draw a line through each letter used.

The Memory Game

LEARNING OBJECTIVES

- to spell words
- to write spelling words correctly
- to match words

SKILLS PRACTICED

- spelling
- writing words
- reading spelling words
- matching words

MATERIALS NEEDED

- TURBO TWIST® Spelling
- a copy of the Memory Game (page 29) for each pair
- pencils
- scissors

PREPARATION

Make one copy of the Memory Game on page 29 for each pair of students.

PREP TIME

5 minutes

DURATION OF ACTIVITY

20 minutes

SKILL LEVEL

Beginner

PLAYERS

2

DIRECTIONS

1. Put students in pairs. Then have one student from each pair cut out the Memory Game cards while the other chooses the Secret Word mode on TURBO TWIST Spelling.

2. Help students select an appropriate skill level on TURBO TWIST Spelling.

3. Invite Player 1 to solve the first secret word. Instruct the student to write the same secret word on two blank Memory Game cards.

4. Have students take turns using TURBO TWIST Spelling and writing their words on the blank Memory Game cards. Remind students to check their written work for correct spelling.

5. Once students have finished filling in all the Memory Game cards, tell them how to play the Memory Game.

   a. Have students mix up the Memory Game cards and place them face down on a table in rows and columns.

   b. Invite Player 1 to turn over two cards, looking for a match. If he or she finds matching word cards, the cards are kept. If he or she does not find matching cards, the cards are put back in the same spots on the table.

   c. The players take turns until all matches are found. The player with the most cards wins.

VARIATIONS

- Students may use their words in sentences after they have completed the Memory Game.

- Students may use TURBO TWIST Spelling to accumulate more than 20 Memory Game cards and play the Memory Game with more word cards.

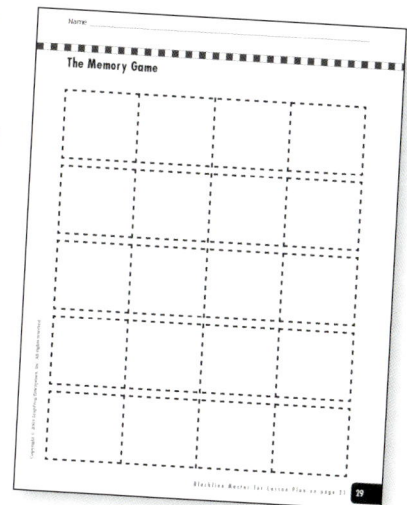

Spelling Word Search Puzzle

LEARNING OBJECTIVES
- to spell words
- to write spelling words

SKILLS PRACTICED
- spelling
- identifying spelling words

MATERIALS NEEDED
- TURBO TWIST® Spelling
- copy of the Spelling Word Search Puzzle Grid (page 30) for each student
- pencils

PREPARATION
Make a copy of the Spelling Word Search Puzzle Grid on page 30 for each student.

PREP TIME
5 minutes

DURATION OF ACTIVITY
20–30 minutes

SKILL LEVEL
All levels

PLAYERS
2

DIRECTIONS

1. Have one student turn on TURBO TWIST Spelling and select the MultiPlayer mode.

2. Then, both students can decide on an appropriate skill level to use for MultiPlayer.

3. Player 1 can begin by entering 2 as the number of players. Then, he or she spells the first word given and records the correct spelling of that word in the word bank at the top of the Word Search Puzzle Grid sheet.

4. Have students follow the TURBO TWIST Spelling directions. Player 2 will spell the next word given. Play continues until each student has six words recorded in his or her word bank.

5. Explain to students how to place the words from their word banks into the puzzle to create a word search puzzle. Students will need to write extra letters in the empty boxes around each of the spelling words so that all boxes in the puzzle grid are filled.

6. Invite students to exchange their Word Search Puzzle Grids. Challenge them to find and circle all the words from the word bank.

VARIATION

- Students can continue play and include more words in their word banks before making the puzzle grid.

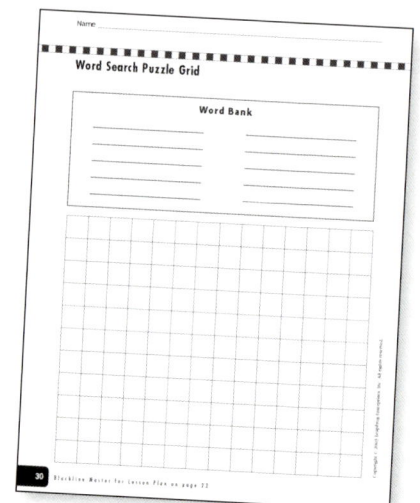

Team Challenge

LEARNING OBJECTIVES

- to practice spelling various words
- to use spelling words in complete sentences

SKILLS PRACTICED

- spelling
- word comprehension
- sentence writing

MATERIALS NEEDED

- TURBO TWIST® Spelling
- a copy of the Team Challenge Record Sheet (page 31) for each team
- several sheets of writing paper
- pencils

PREPARATION

Make a copy of the Team Challenge Record Sheet on page 31 for each team.

PREP TIME

5 minutes

DURATION OF ACTIVITY

15–25 minutes

SKILL LEVEL

Beginner/Intermediate

PLAYERS

2–4 students per group

DIRECTIONS

1. Ask students to choose the MultiPlayer mode and an appropriate skill level on TURBO TWIST Spelling.

2. Explain that each team takes a turn spelling the words prompted by TURBO TWIST Spelling and writes them correctly on their Team Challenge Record Sheet. Teams record a point on their record sheet if one of their players spells the word correctly.

3. Tell students that teams should continue spelling words and recording points for words spelled correctly until one team has ten points. Then, TURBO TWIST Spelling should be set aside.

4. Have each team use the words on their record sheet to write five complete sentences.

5. Ask a volunteer from each team to read their sentences aloud.

VARIATIONS

- Teams may work together to use all the words from the record sheets in five sentences.

- Teams can extend the activity by writing their words in alphabetical order.

- As an alternative to writing sentences, teams can use their words to write about a particular current event.

Home-School Connection

MAKING A HOME-SCHOOL CONNECTION WITH TURBO TWIST® SPELLING

As a teacher, you know how important it is for parents and teachers to work together as a team to foster students' learning. Building that bridge between home and school can really make a difference in a student's education. TURBO TWIST Spelling provides an opportunity for students to review information at home that has been taught in the classroom. At home, your student can use TURBO TWIST Spelling to reinforce and practice what he or she learned in school that very day.

It's easy to send TURBO TWIST Spelling home to provide the kind of practice and reinforcement that is necessary for students to master new skills. Because TURBO TWIST Spelling provides a highly motivating and rewarding experience through its multisensory approach, parents may find their children far more eager to practice spelling skills at home.

TURBO TWIST Spelling can be used with very little assistance. That makes it a great tool for your remedial and special-needs students. Send it home with them so they get the additional practice they need.

To introduce parents to TURBO TWIST Spelling and the learning opportunities it offers, you can introduce it at an open house. A fun way to do this

would be to have a group of parents play the MultiPlayer mode. They could play in teams to test their own spelling skills and thus see firsthand how challenging and rewarding TURBO TWIST Spelling can be.

Another option is to send TURBO TWIST Spelling home as a homework assignment. Perhaps one of your students is struggling with spelling. You could instruct your student to use the Learn It! mode starting at a particular level and challenge the student to write on paper each word presented. Have the student continue at this level until he or she spells each word correctly.

Or, ask a student to take TURBO TWIST Spelling home, write down ten new spelling words learned while playing the device, and be ready to help teach the class these words the next day in school.

Use the sign-out sheet at the back of the Teacher's Manual to keep track of when students have borrowed a TURBO TWIST Spelling and when it's due back. In addition to sending your student home with TURBO TWIST Spelling, have them also take the Letter to Parents on the next page. This will provide parents with a general introduction to the device and offer suggestions for educational activities parents and their children can do together.

Dear Parents,

At school, your child is working with TURBO TWIST® Spelling to practice important spelling skills and rules. This interactive tool from LeapFrog SchoolHouse is designed to make spelling practice both engaging and effective.

TURBO TWIST Spelling offers various spelling games that keep your child interested. Your child can learn from five different study modes. In Learn It! he or she will learn how to spell different words based on skill level. When using Missing Letter, your child will fill in missing letters to spell level-appropriate words. Spell It! will challenge your child to spell whole words. In Secret Word, your child has to guess the correct letters to spell a secret word that is only identified by the number of letters it has. A lively mode called MultiPlayer is designed for groups of two, three, or four players who are looking for a good challenge. Players spell words and compete for "brain cells."

TURBO TWIST Spelling can help you build that important bridge between home and school. At home, your child can use TURBO TWIST Spelling to reinforce and practice what he or she learned in school that very day.

And you can join in on the learning and help your child develop his or her spelling skills. There are many activities using TURBO TWIST Spelling that you and your child can do together. Here are some activities that may be completed together by students and their families to practice important spelling skills and rules:

Add a Letter (2 or more players)

Materials: TURBO TWIST Spelling, paper and pencil for scorekeeping

1. Player 1 activates and sets TURBO TWIST Spelling to the Spell It! mode. After hearing the spelling word, Player 1 inputs the first letter. If this letter is correct, he or she passes TURBO TWIST Spelling to the next player, who inputs the second letter, and so on. If the letter is incorrect, Player 2 guesses the letter.

2. If the group spells the word correctly, everyone gets a point. If an error is made, only the players who input a correct letter get a point. The first player to score ten points is the winner.

Two-Minute Time (2 or more players)

Materials: TURBO TWIST Spelling, timer, paper and pencil for scorekeeping

1. Player 1 activates and sets TURBO TWIST Spelling to the Spell It! mode. Player 2 sets the timer for two minutes and keeps score. Player 2 will record the number of words that Player 1 is able to spell using TURBO TWIST Spelling in the two-minute time period. Player 1 receives one point for each word spelled correctly in the two-minute time period.

2. Next, Player 2 sees how many words he or she can correctly spell in the specified two-minute time period, while Player 1 records the number of words spelled correctly. (If more than two players are in the game, take turns so everyone gets a chance to spell and keep time.)

3. The first player to reach ten points wins the game.

Tell Me a Story (2 or more players)

Materials: TURBO TWIST Spelling, paper, pencil

1. Players choose the Learn It! mode on TURBO TWIST Spelling.

2. The first player copies the given word and writes a complete sentence using the word.

3. The other players take their turns.

4. The group works together to create a cooperative story using all the words written.

These are just a few of the games your child can play at home with you to reinforce and practice important spelling skills being taught in the classroom.

To get more information about TURBO TWIST Spelling, visit the LeapFrog Web site at **www.leapfrog.com**.

Sincerely,

_____

and LeapFrog SchoolHouse

Name _____

Leaping Lily Pads Game Board

Start

You catch your favorite bug! Move ahead two.

You taught a friend how to improve her jumping power. Take an extra turn.

Your croaking earns the compliments of a fisher. Move ahead one.

You have to hide from an alligator. Miss a turn.

You can't shake the hiccups. Go back two.

Bubba's
Welcome to Bubba's Buggy Diner—where everything is guaranteed to be delicious!

Your froggy little sister pushed you off the lily pad. Go back two.

You win tickets to the Frog Fair. Move ahead two.

Blackline Master for Lesson Plan on page 18

Build a Robot

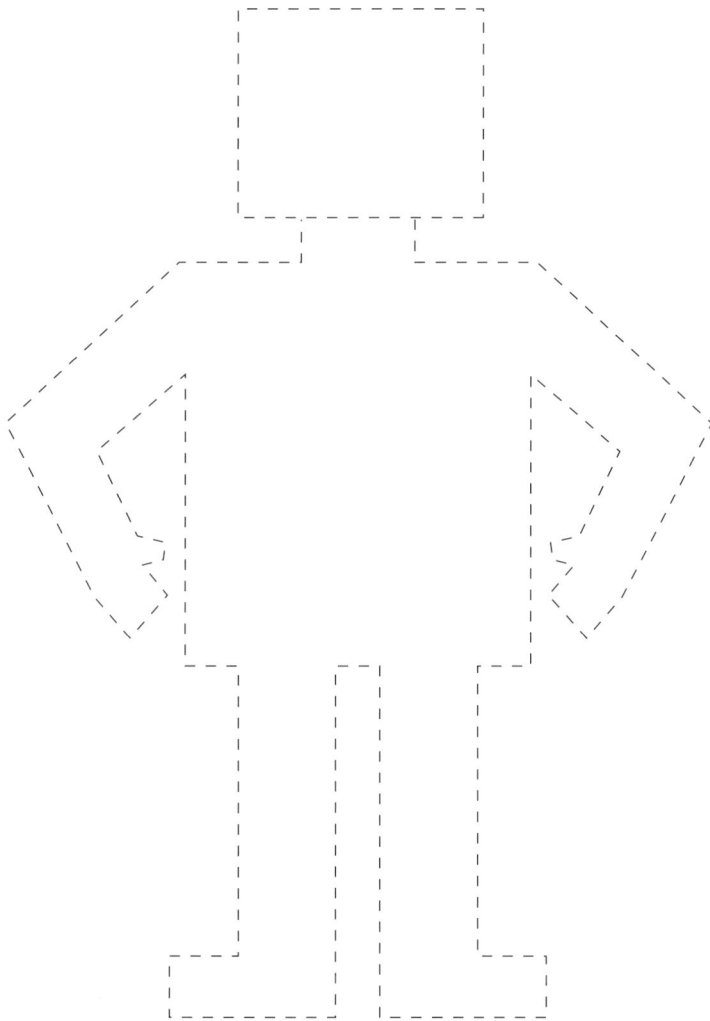

Add these things to build the robot. Go down the list in order. Draw the part(s) each time you miss a letter.

1. head
2. body
3. legs (both)
4. arms (both)
5. feet (both)
6. hands (both)
7. facial features (eyes, mouth, nose)
8. hat

Incorrect Letters

_____   _____   _____   _____

_____   _____   _____   _____

Name _____

Cut and Choose

A	A	B	B	C	C	D	D
E	E	F	F	G	G	H	H
I	I	J	J	K	K	L	L
M	M	N	N	O	O	P	P
Q	Q	R	R	S	S	T	T
U	U	V	V	W	W	X	X
		Y	Y	Z	Z		

Blackline Master for Lesson Plan on page 20

Name _____

The Memory Game

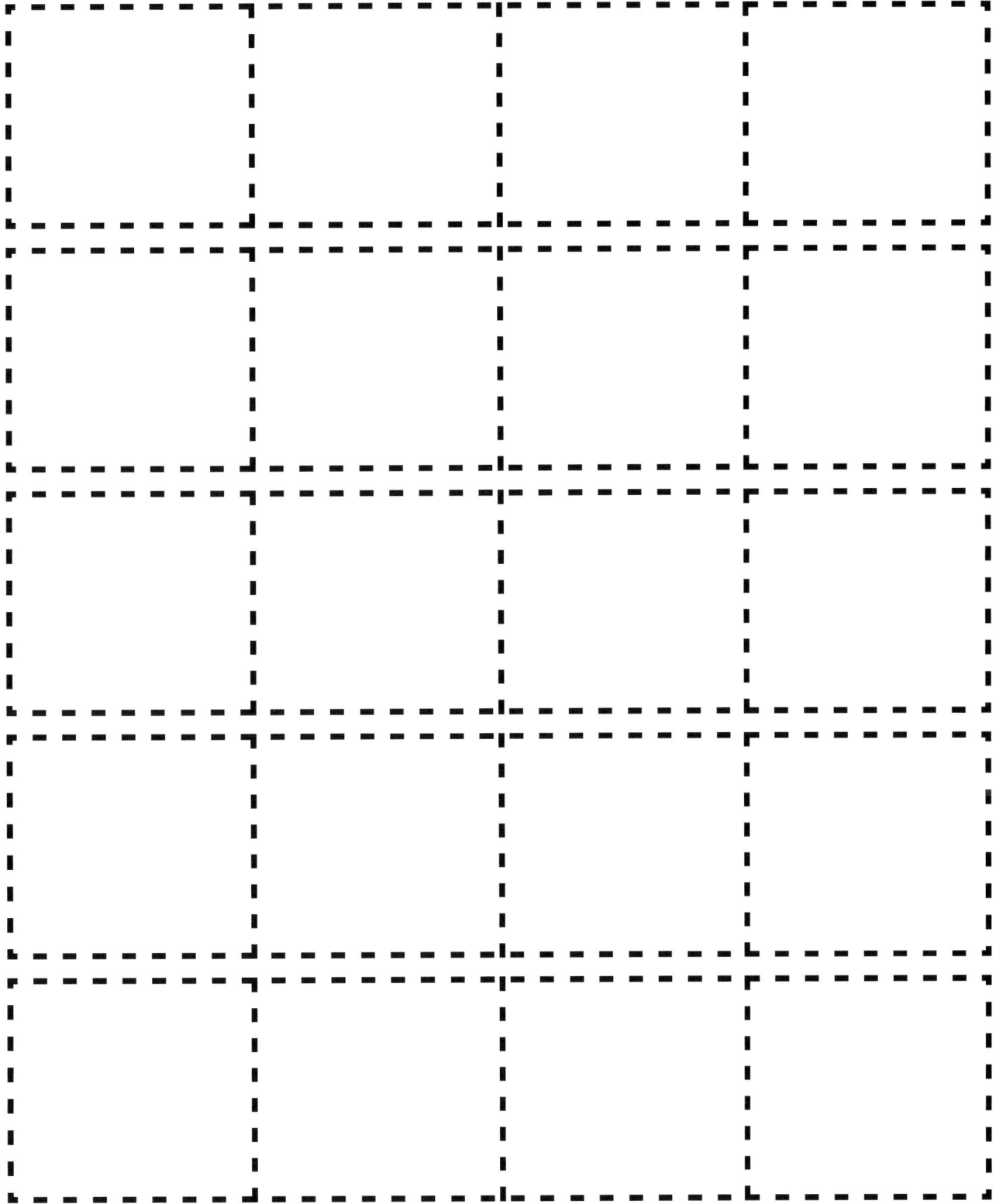

Word Search Puzzle Grid

Word Bank

_____   _____

_____   _____

_____   _____

_____   _____

_____   _____

Name _____

Team Challenge Record Sheet

Word	Spelled Correctly 1 point	Spelled Incorrectly 0 points

Date _____

Teacher Organizer
Home-School Connection

Name of Student	Date Borrowed	Date Returned	Notes

Name _____   Date _____

Student Organizer
Activities I've Played

Name of Mode	Date Played	Level Played	Score Earned
1.			
2.			
3.			
4.			
5.			
6.			
7.			
8.			
9.			
10.			
11.			
12.			
13.			
14.			
15.			

Base Unit Information

DEVICE INFORMATION: A DESCRIPTION OF BASE UNIT SKILL LEVELS

TURBO TWIST Spelling offers 33 levels of activities that can be played without the use of a cartridge. To practice a particular skill without the use of a cartridge, find the skill on the chart below to identify the corresponding skill level. Then, use the manual level change option to enter the selected level and start playing.

GRADE	SKILL LEVEL	SKILL	SAMPLE WORDS
GRADE 1	1	Words with Short a Words with Short e Words with Short i Words with Short o	had bed it box
	2	Words with Short u Consonant Blends with s Consonant Blends with l Consonant Blends with r	up step glad grip
	3	Words with Long a Words with Long e Words with Long i Words with Long o	name me time note
	4	Words with Long u Consonant Combination sh Consonant Combination th	mule ship thin
	5	Consonant Combinations ch, tch More Words with Long a More Words with Long i More Words with Long o	chin sail pipe soak
GRADE 2	6	More Words with the ow Sound Consonant Blends ng and nk Words with a Double Consonant at the End Words That Are Not Spelled the Way They Sound	how bank toss want
	7	Words with the k Sound Words with Long a Words with Long e Words with Long i	kid day sea my
	8	Words with Long o Words with Long u Words That Begin with qu or squ	goat hoop squeak
	9	Compound Words Adding ed or ing to Words Adding s or es to Words More Words That Are Not Spelled the Way They Sound	outside saved banks again
	10	Consonant Combination wh Words with the ar Sound Words with the or Sound Two-Syllable Words with Short Vowels	when art more cabin
GRADE 3	11	Words with the ow Sound Words with the oy Sound Three-Letter Consonant Blends Words with Long a	town toy scrap pave
	12	Words with Long e Words with Long i Words with Long o	heat fight soap
	13	Words with the Vowel Sound in book, hoop, or huge Words That End with the j or s Sound Words with the Schwa Sound Words with the aw Sound	pool page awake talk
	14	Words That Are Not Spelled the Way They Sound Homophones (Words That Sound the Same) More Consonant Blends and Combinations	friend ate drain
	15	Words with Silent k or Silent w Words with the ow or oy Sound Words with a Double Consonant in the Middle Adding ed or ing to Words	knee void summer shaded
	16	Plural Forms of Nouns Unusual Plurals Adding er or est to Adjectives	parties calves funnier

GRADE	SKILL LEVEL	SKILL	SAMPLE WORDS
GRADE 4	17	Words with the Prefix un- or re- Words with Long a Words with Long e	unfair stray chief
	18	Words with Long i Words with Long o Words with the Vowel Sound in book, hoop, or huge Words with the ar or air Sound	tight bowl fruit glare
	19	Words with the or Sound Words with the ur Sound Words with the eer Sound	court firm near
	20	Words with the j Sound Words with the Schwa Sound (Unstressed uh Sound) Words with the Schwa Sound and l or r	giant afford model
	21	Words with the Schwa Sound and n Words with the aw Sound Three-Syllable Words Words in Which the c Makes the s Sound	kitchen launch electric cycle
	22	Words with the Prefix mis-,dis-, in-, un-, or re- Words with the Suffix –ful or –less Words with the Suffix -ness, -ment, or -ly	react careful stillness
GRADE 5	23	Words with Silent Letters Words with the aw, oi, or ow Sound Words with the air, ar, or or Sound	thumb tower aware
	24	Words with the ur or eer Sound Words with the Schwa Sound (Unstressed uh Sound) Words with the Schwa Sound Followed by l, n, or r Compound Words	fierce alert visor whatever
	25	Words with the sh or ch Sound Words with the k, the s, or the j Sound Words with the f Sound	patient package rough
	26	Homophones (Words That Sound the Same) Words with the Prefix pre-, re-, post-, or co- Words with the Prefix dis-, in-, im-, non-, or un- Words with the Prefix bi-, mid-, semi-, or tri-	vain preview impolite tricycle
	27	Words with ie or ei Words That Are Not Spelled the Way They Sound Words with the Suffix -ful, -less, -ment, or -ness Words with the Suffix -ion, -tion, or -sion	grief pretty luckless division
	28	Words with the Suffix -ent, -ant, -able, or -ible Three-Syllable and Four-Syllable Words Words with a Greek or a Latin Root	vacant territory erupt
GRADE 6	29	Compound Words Words with a Vowel Plus r Words with the Schwa Sound (Unstressed uh Sound) Final Schwa + r	backlash categorical adequacy gossamer
	30	Final Schwa + n or l Homophones Adding -ed and -ing Consonant Blends and Combinations	alluvial hostel acquiring government
	31	Words with the /f/ Sound, the /z/ Sound, or the /zh/ Sound in fusion Double Consonants Endings -ion, -tion, -sion Suffixes -ent, -ant, -able, -ible	lozenge grommet incision congruent
	32	Suffixes -ance, -ence, -ate Spelling the sh Sound Prefixes super-, sub-, inter-, intra-	inanimate crustacean interstellar
	33	Negative Prefixes Prefixes per-, pre-, pro- Words from Greek and Latin Words from Other Languages Words That Are Not Spelled the Way They Sound	infrequent perforate bellicose soprano circuitry

CARE AND MAINTENANCE

Caring for your TURBO TWIST® handheld:
• Keep away from food and beverages.
• Clean with a slightly damp cloth. Never submerge the TURBO TWIST handheld in water.
• Remove batteries for prolonged storage.
• Avoid extreme temperatures.

BATTERY

Battery Installation:
1. Requires 4 "AA" (called LR6 in some countries) alkaline batteries.
2. When the batteries run low on power, the device's speech may become garbled or it may repeat itself. Replace the batteries at this time.
3. Open the battery door with a screwdriver.
4. Install new batteries as shown in the polarity diagram (+/−) inside the battery compartment.
5. Replace battery door securely.

Battery Safety:
• Batteries are small objects. Replacement of batteries must be done by adults.
• Follow the polarity (+/−) diagram in the battery compartment.
• Promptly remove dead batteries from the device. Dispose of used batteries properly.
• DO NOT incinerate used batteries.
• DO NOT dispose of batteries in fire, as batteries may explode or leak.
• DO NOT mix old and new batteries or types of batteries (i.e., alkaline/standard).
• DO NOT use rechargeable batteries.
• DO NOT recharge non-rechargeable batteries.
• DO NOT short-circuit the supply terminals.

TROUBLESHOOTING

Symptom:	Try This:
Device does not turn on or does not respond.	• Remove batteries and put them back in. • Make sure battery cover is correctly secured. • Clean battery contacts with rubbing alcohol. • Install new batteries.
Device makes strange sounds or behaves erratically.	• Install new batteries.
Device makes improper responses.	• Install new batteries.

For additional service or product information, please call LeapFrog SchoolHouse Customer Service at (800) 883-7430.

NOTE: This device complies with Part 15 of the FCC rules. This equipment has been tested and found to comply with the limits for a Class B digital device pursuant to Part 15 of the FCC rules. These limits are designed to provide reasonable protection against harmful interference to radio communications. Because this product generates, uses, and can radiate radio frequency energy, there can be no guarantee that interference will not occur. If this product does cause interference to radio or television reception (you can check this by turning the product off and on while listening for the interference), one or more of the following measures may be useful:
• Reorient or relocate the receiving antenna.
• Increase the separation between the product and the radio or the TV.
• Consult the dealer or an experienced TV-radio technician for help.

LEAPFROG ENTERPRISES, INC. WARRANTY

This product from LeapFrog SchoolHouse, a division of LeapFrog Enterprises, Inc. ("LeapFrog") is warranted to only the original purchaser for a period of one year from the original purchase date, under normal use and service, against defective workmanship and material. This warranty is void if the product has been damaged by accident or other unreasonable use, immersion in water, neglect, abuse, battery leakage or improper installation, improper service, or other causes not arising out of defects in workmanship or materials. Repair or replacement as provided under this warranty is the exclusive remedy of the purchaser. LeapFrog and its affiliates shall not be liable for any incidental or consequential damage for breach of any express warranty on this product. Any implied warranty of merchantability or fitness for a particular purpose on this product limited to the duration of this warranty. Some states do not allow the exclusion of limitation of incidental or consequential damages, or limitation on how long an implied warranty lasts, so the above limitations or exclusions may not apply to you. This warranty gives you specific legal rights and you may also have other rights, which vary from state to state.

During the warranty period, your product will either be repaired or replaced at LeapFrog's option, when returned, shipping prepaid and with proof of purchase date as instructed by a LeapFrog service representative. In the event that your product is replaced, the replacement product will be continued under the original warranty or for 30 days, whichever is longer.

Product design subject to change.

TURBO TWIST, QUANTUM LEAP, and the Quantum Leap logo are registered trademarks of LeapFrog Enterprises, Inc.

To learn about other LeapFrog SchoolHouse products, visit www.LeapFrogSchoolHouse.com.